The Poetry & Lyrics of Jay Semko

by

Jay Semko

A WOOD DRAGON BOOK

All rights reserved. This book or any portion thereof may not be reproduced in part or in whole without the express written permission of the author except for the use of brief quotations in a critical review.

Copyright 2021 Jay Semko
Cover art: Callum Jagger
Poet's Photo: Randy Woods

Published by:
Wood Dragon Books
Post Office Box 429
Mossbank, Saskatchewan, Canada S0H3G0
www.wooddragonbooks.com

Available in paperback, hardcover, eBook and audiobook.

Library and Archives Canada Cataloguing in Publication
Semko, Jay, 1960–
ISBN: 978-1-989078-63-1

For information about Jay Semko: www.jaysemko.com
To contact Jay regarding speaking or performing:
jaysemko@gmail.com

God is in the music and the music loves you

JAY SEMKO

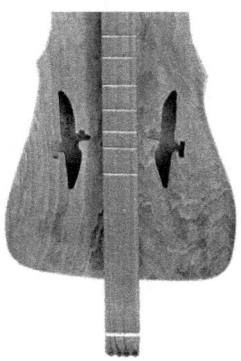

Table of Contents

	Notes from the Poet	1
	Introduction	3
1	Below the Equator	11
2	Solid as Steel	13
3	Adventure on My Breath	15
4	Helsinki on the Mainline	17
5	No Rabies Necessary	19
6	Lullabies	21
7	My Mother in the Hospital	23
8	Make It Through To Sunrise	32
9	The Hand from the Sky	34
10	Lake of Mud	36
11	Rob Roy Room	38
12	Come Across the Water	40
13	Junkie Pride	42
14	This Rage	44
15	Send the Saints	46
16	International Superstar	48
17	Heartaches and Numbers	50
18	The Sadness is Strong	52
19	Men's Wing Christmas	54
20	Spaghetti Western	55
21	The Win	57
22	Clean	58
23	More Ferocious in Toronto	60
24	Rode In On	62
25	Unsuccessful Son	65
26	Lifetime Plan	67
27	Who Cares (Unemployed)	68
28	Too Long	70
29	Sagging Sunday	71
30	Mouse in a Hole	72
31	New Day	76
32	Surrounded By Love	77
33	Sending Love	80

34	Redberry (love song to a lake)	81
35	Macramé	83
36	Sizzle Magoo	84
37	Let the Love In	85
38	Flora Vista	87
39	Diving In So Deep	89
40	For Certain	91
41	Sweet Sweet Love	92
42	Before You Leave Canada	94
43	The Moon The Stars and You	96
44	Drop You in the Water	97
45	Jesus is Gonna Help Me	99
46	Gospel	101
47	Asleep in the Loving Arms of God	103
48	For The Love Of A Word	105
49	God's Daughter	107
	Albums	111

Notes from the Poet

Songs are meant to be sung … poems are meant to be read.

This book is a collection and a mixture of song lyrics and 'stand alone' poems written over a 25-year period. The lyrics included have been selected from solo recordings I have released and many of them have been adapted for the written page, as sometimes they 'sing' better than they 'look'.

Compiling this collection has been an emotional experience for me. Lots of memories—many intense feelings—a combo of stream-of-consciousness and tightly constructed song lyrics with a healthy dose of 'in-betweenness' (that's an interesting word isn't it?)

It is my hope that the reader will enjoy joining me and my thoughts, feelings, and quirks as we stumble and sway our way together down the daily roads we wander … so let's go wandering ….

Introduction

Words can be missiles—missiles can carry weapons or confetti or food or love or hope or sadness or strength or inane observational frequencies of affection or depression.

Combine words with music and it's a whole other world … and as important as words are in conjunction with music and how this potentially potent combination can go straight to your heart or your gut or any other anatomical area, the music will generally always lead the way. That is the amazing and undefinable element of a song, and why we crave hearing some of them over and over.

I was an early writer and reader. When IQ and other tests were conducted at the beginning of Grade 2, it was discovered that I had a college level reading, writing and comprehension ability. I wasn't told this at the time in 1967, and didn't learn this information until many years later. I did know that I loved to read and to make up rhymes, and to invent tunes and melodies that I noodled around with on the piano at my grandparents' house.

My family lived on a farm a few miles outside of Saskatoon, Saskatchewan, in the heart of the 'wheat belt'—also known as 'Canada's breadbasket.' We moved there from the city of Saskatoon when I was a few months into Grade 1. My cousins lived on the farm down the path from us and my mom's parents lived down the other path from us. My sister, my cousins, and I—known as the 'city slickers'—rode the school bus every day. We endured massive relentless bullying on our daily hell rides (first on the route to be picked up—last to be dropped off).

During that time there were certainly no advanced learning or accelerated programs, so the scholastic 'powers that be' moved me from Grade 2 to Grade 4.

I 'skipped' Grade 3, which unfortunately had the effect of making me even more of a freak outcast and easy target for bullies. Inexpensive piano lessons were offered at the school, and my folks signed me up with hopes that I could transfer my sense of melody into the world of Bach, Beethoven or Liberace. Alas, this was not to be—I was quite simply unable to read musical notation with any level of proficiency, no matter how hard I tried. I spent hours in tears and frustration at the keyboard residing at my grandparents' house where I would walk nightly for piano practice and after a couple of years the piano lessons were abandoned.

I continued my noodling and became a decent 'by ear' player with my own mutant style, which continues to this day. Around this time, I became interested in the guitar. My dad was attempting to learn how to play, with a beginner acoustic guitar and 'learn how to play' chord books purchased from either Gordie Brandt's or Colliers, two of the local Saskatoon music stores. I found I was able to put the lyrics of the songs and the chords in the books together (actually quite an epiphany to me at the time) and begin my painful first attempts at forming chords, replete with the necessary fingertip pain and blisters, and the seemingly endless patience required of a pre-adolescent boy.

I loved the songs on the radio—the way the words and the music worked together were fascinating to me—and I memorized the words to all the radio hits of the late sixties, listening deep into the night on my little transistor radio. I was a lonely boy with few friends and a deep inferiority complex—books and music were everything to me. (I tried to play sports and eventually achieved some proficiency at some of them—I desperately wanted to fit in but never did.) However ... solitude and loneliness can sometimes be one's best friends, although I definitely didn't realize it at the time. I made up stories and poems, fantasized about almost everything, and lo and behold, developed my IMAGINATION.

Every Saturday, my folks would take me into Saskatoon

for swimming lessons at the YMCA. One day, as I was waiting for one of them after the lesson, I noticed an ad for guitar lessons being taught at the Y. I was excited about this, convinced my parents that this was a good idea and began the ten weeks of lessons soon after. The guitar teacher was a somewhat scary-looking man with a pronounced scar on his cheek. At the start of the first lesson, he pointed to it, and sternly said, "You see this scar? This is what happens when you lean over the top of your guitar when you're changing strings and one of them breaks—NEVER DO THAT!" And I never did.

I loved the lessons—I was learning SONGS! At the end of the ten-week course, for the informal 'recital', I played Ian Tyson's *Four Strong Winds*. I didn't sing, but I could hear the words in my head. From there my life changed; I was hooked on music, and in particular, SONGS.

When I was in Grade 7, my family moved to Saskatoon. It was really the beginning of Part 2 of my childhood, a fresh start for me in many ways. The inferiority complex, shyness, and desire for invisibility was still there, but some things changed. Instead of accepting the beatings and abuse I had learned to withstand during my years at the rural school, I began to fight back—and fight back I did. I realized that, at least on the surface and in the context of dealing with other humans, I didn't feel the fear I had previously experienced, and when I was physically challenged by bullies or other boys testing me—my fists, and indeed every part of my body, went into action. I never looked for fights, but from that time I have never been afraid to defend myself vigorously when necessary.

I took guitar and bass lessons at Gordie Brandt's Music. The Brandt family lived on the same block as my family (one of many fortuitous things that contributed to my musical development). There was always music coming from the open windows of their house during the summer months. They were wonderfully kind and encouraging people who became good friends.

High school was a different world—a large school with kids from many different areas of the city. By this time, I was obsessed with rock music and I practiced intensely with the hopes of joining or starting the next Beatles or Rolling Stones. Bands were formed and disbanded, and a whole other side of education occurred for me—which included drugs and alcohol.

I remember one teacher, Mr. Lee, who praised my poetry in his English class, and it really helped my confidence when it came to writing—thank you Mr. Lee.

I was learning to write lyrics by osmosis. "If you hang around a barber shop long enough you'll eventually get a haircut," as they say. My first songwriting attempts, in my last year of high school, were, quite simply, horrible and horribly derivative. It would be a few years before I really found my own voice with my lyrics. Numerous bands I was in, playing songs written by others, with occasional incursions into original songwriting, contributed to my education as a songwriter/lyricist.

During this time, I was writing down my most personal thoughts and feelings—poems, random scribbles, scattered ideas and mental gymnastic experiments—without really considering they could become song lyrics. Eventually I began to incorporate these thoughts and feelings into my lyrics, and voilà, better and more emotionally engaging songs emerged.

After many bands came and went, and many songs were written, The Northern Pikes were born. Although we were young (I was age 23 in 1984 when the band began), we were musical veterans with many years of touring and recording experience. At first I was the principal songwriter—I encouraged Merl (Bryck) and Bryan (Potvin) to write more, and indeed they did, with the band eventually becoming a triple songwriter, triple singer powerhouse with drummer Don (Schmid) contributing to the band songwriting as well.

And I simply just kept on writing ... words for songs,

words for comfort, words for anger, words for joy, words for sadness, words for the deep loneliness that lingered for so long ... words, precious words.

This is how this book started—the seeds were planted many years ago, and the roots are very deep.

We were (and are) a very good band. We released two independent albums in the mid-'80s and then were signed to Virgin Records, where our music career rose to another level. We have written, recorded and released, as of this writing, 14 albums, selling over a million worldwide which have included numerous Canadian hit singles, and have toured extensively in Canada, the USA, and Japan. I have personally released ten solo albums and simultaneously developed a career as a music composer for film and television, working on the syndicated series *Due South*, and many others.

I have never stopped writing poetry. Sometimes the poems become songs, sometimes the poems become different poems, sometimes they languish in the hinterland of maybes and notebooks and hen scratch thoughts and feelings spewed onto a page, a receipt, or a parking ticket.

Life's ups and downs happen ... and I believe everything happens for a reason.

A huge part of my life, which you will discover when you read the poetry in this book, has been my experiences and challenges with mental health and addiction. I am a recovering addict (a term which I consider includes my addiction to alcohol) living with Bipolar Disorder. In recent years, I have become more open and vocal about these once-taboo subjects which now, quite frankly, I sometimes just won't stop talking about.

Writing is everything to me (almost ...). It is my mental massage, my psychotherapy, my friend, and often my connection/conduit to spirit and soul.

I have often considered putting my poetry into the world—friends have suggested this, and I have largely responded with, "Yes—good idea—maybe someday …."

Well, someday has arrived.

In 2018, I suffered a painful relapse with substances and ended up having a one-week stay in a detox facility and a subsequent two-month stay in a treatment centre. I have had previous stays in detox, rehab and psychiatric centres, but this was the most painful, as I had relapsed after ten years of continuous sobriety. I was one of the oldest individuals at the facility. It was sometimes quite challenging, but during my stay there I came to the realization that it is crucial to my mental health and sobriety to continue to 'put it all down' on the page. I consider myself an ongoing work-in-progress. I learned an awful lot during those two months, and I wish I could say that I lived happily ever after and everything has been pretty peachy since then but … hey it's called "**Life**". I need to show up for it *every day*, and I need to put the work in to maintain my mental health and sobriety *every day*.

In the autumn of 2017, The Northern Pikes began a cross-Canada tour in celebration of the 30-year anniversary of the release of our first album on Virgin Records, *"Big Blue Sky"*. It was our first chronological national tour in many years, and at every venue there was an information booth from CAMH (The Centre for Addiction and Mental Health). I have spoken openly in the past about my addiction and mental health challenges, and it was a good opportunity to bring more awareness to our audiences and to help reduce the stigma that still exists concerning these subjects.

During each concert, I would take a few minutes to speak briefly about my journey and inform the audience about the CAMH booth in the theatre lobby where they could get more information. After each show on the tour the band would gather at our merchandise table, usually located near the CAMH booth, to 'meet and greet' the fans who wanted to meet us, say hello after many years, ask us to sign albums, or purchase memorabilia. During these 'meet and greets', I met many people who would thank me for sharing some of my journey through mental health and addiction challenges, and who would tell me, often quite emotionally, about their own personal challenges regarding themselves and their friends and loved ones. This made every 'meet and greet' a very emotional event for me, and it confirmed and reaffirmed the importance of sharing my story with the possibility of potentially helping others. I was amazed at how many folks had gone through, or were going through, similar experiences, and as a result, I resolved to be even more vocal about this. One can feel extremely alone in this world, and if I can contribute in some way to possibly help someone somewhere to not feel so alone, I will do it. It helps me immensely, and is crucial to my own personal recovery.

Life ... yes, it continues and I am very grateful for every moment, no matter what that moment may bring ... the illness and passing of my mother during the Pikes 2017 tour ("My Mother in the Hospital") ... the death of my dog *Lady* in 2020 and good old frightening mortality ("Send the Saints") ... Christmas 2018 in rehab ("Men's Wing Christmas") ... addiction—well there's a few of those here ... spirituality, love, lakes, drunkalogues, depression, Jesus, hope, and a few other things. Welcome aboard—let's go on a trip.

Below the Equator

tuning you in on the satellite dish
the second or third of all my wishes
wind's coming up
sky's turning green
birds are all FREAKING OUT

cupboard full of coins
singer on the radio
sad refrains
over and over and over
again

I thought about leaving but where would I go?
edge of the lake
north and the snow
to the cool blue water
below the equator

clear the deck of rotting corpses
New Year's Day is here again
winter on the night shift justifies and stupefies
with ABSOLUTENESS

hold the hoof of the frightened doe
"we just wanna eat the grass and the leaves"

the odyssey continues
ghosts of the deer I have killed on the highway
will come back to haunt me when I least expect it

they do not speak or make a sound

they just look at me with those big deer eyes
wondering
"why am I not running through fields and forests?
oh, the shame of the creature who sent me to Heaven!"

I'd be wise to keep my eyes on the road
listen to gospel
stay in the veins
be all and everyone I am fully meant to be

below the equator

Solid as Steel
---

solid as steel
soft as the dawn

Chinese paintings on the wall
keep praying
hands unfolded
golden goose with a sign on the window
"NO FLYERS NO SALESMEN"

this runaway air conditioner freeway
will be the sound thrusting me over the waterfall

"well, hello there young fella"

don't think it's rained here for centuries
but I really don't mind

I see my life shaking like a branch in a gale

faith in God
faith in love

soft as sundown
solid as steel

make up new words
draw a new roadmap
they changed all the signs
moved all the landmarks

once they were wheat fields
now they're old oil wells
where are the windmills?
where are the children?

well on our way in the 21st century
the age of the famous and futile

I kneel on the ground
listen to God
talk to the sand
raise up my hands to the blue prairie sky

LOVE all the things that brought me this far
LOVE all the people who make it so hard
THROW down the burdens right there at the roadside
BRING along water
because you're gonna need it

East Germany on a globe from the sixties
with all of the world of my childhood on PAUSE

no more tape
only air
wind
sun

"it's all for the good of us all"… as they say

solid as steel
soft
as the moonlight

Adventure on My Breath

I shouted at the open plains
with the voice of a lion
inside my head

ice crystals shimmered
shifted

I knew I was not dead yet

I picked at the bones of my new complacency
the old fighter shrieking at the ringside
cleaning up the bloody mess after it was over

white knuckles
memory of a victory

Siberia

at least that's how it seems
in a greyhound skating down a highway

everyone sleeps in the comfort of their daily lives
but I'm awake
with adventure on my breath

what is this muse
sending inspiration
when depression tries to shake us from our shells

we beat our fists against our chests
without a meaning

when it's over we are bruised
embarrassed

I had a lover once
love without a consummation

she was tender
hard on the outside

my wanderlust
and years without a word from me
sent her far away with sadness
but never bitter

now I'm wide awake

there is a power that pounds on the door
of restless nights

sleepwalking
only with a straitjacket

we hug ourselves
kiss ourselves

tell ourselves our deepest secrets
never make a sound

you can slay your dictionaries
you can steal your television vision
you can crave the sleep of the angels

I'm awake
with
adventure on my breath

Helsinki on the Mainline

Helsinki on the mainline
wish away the past

blue light imposes unexpected serenity
on the unsuspecting grateful

I can't dispose of the hamster wheel
inside my head

where the grazing elk standing on the lawn
of a postcard night,
friend of all the disconcerting tragedies of day,
simply munches…
staring blithely into space

she was a waitress—now a server

alcohol served to steal the bravery

still young with glinting eyes and arms
we talked
we drank
we talked some more

when the fatal hour approached
all conversation ceased

we both gazed at the moon
grinning moon
sly moon
then I walked away

sometimes I believe
this is MAGNIFICENCE

bears are freaky
unpredictable

especially up north
in Scandinavia

it's a smooth rumble with eyes closed
yes indeed

Helsinki on the mainline

No Rabies Necessary

solitary

same time every day the orb descends
through wonderful July

tick tick tick goes the cuckoo clock

I still need glasses
I still need exercise
I still need to do
ALL THIS CRAP

and in the back of the brain cave the bats are recharging
with a few

pushups
sit ups
jumping jacks
stretching

patiently waiting

I try not to think about it
but it's
ALWAYS THERE

the endless, deep love
for the things that will KILL ME
no rabies necessary

just the gift of poison
snow white's apple
from the distillery

exclusively for the bats……
they're cute but they bite

don't worry

no rabies necessary

Lullabies

lullabies in a parallel universe

sing low
to soothe

a different time
stronger shoulders
before the war
before the winter
before the wine-soaked sad goodbyes

naked trees
big wind
rain on yellow leaves

this is all
and more today

richest sadness
knowing smiles
drowsy eyes recall the hardest years

soft the sound of the wicked footsteps
trudging the twilight road to Rome

the ship set sail two days ago
with all the prisoners aboard

crimson night
cricket wolves
stars so high you'll never reach them
take a deep breath
hold it tightly
save the promises
we'll keep them

lullabies in a parallel universe

sing low
for the sleepers

My Mother in the Hospital

2017
on a submarine with wheels
with a busload of other ancient former vagabonds
preparing to rock across the nation

I'm with my sister
and my mother
at the doctor's office
after the tests

terminal

weeks?
years?
probably months

I could see the tears welling up
in his eyes
as the news was broken

stunned silence
from the family trio
on the snail ride home

I don't believe it
what do these doctors know anyway??

denial on the day

the slow, stagnant waters of reality
rising up through my bones
arriving in my brain with a million questions

what now?

so depressing

her courage kicked in
it was always there
but now the key was turned
the engine started

911 so many times
the hurried phone call
race to the house
firefighters there first
mom in a daze
poison coursing through her
the stretcher
the IV
the all encompassing
ever demanding
worry

no time for sadness
yet

swamped in the ER
"here—you're her son?
put this in the apple juice
—she needs to drink it or she'll die!!"

me cajoling
convincing
begging her
to take it
her eyes rolling back in her head
here's my chance!!

down the hatch
elixir waterfall down her throat
her half-awake embarrassment
at the inevitable result

then
slowly
coming back

while next door through the curtain
the nurse tells the unbelieving mother
of her child's meth addiction

we're all trying to save someone

in and out of the hospital
I keep hoping for something

I can't believe it
do I just accept this?
NO!!!

home
then hospital
then home
then hospital
then

palliative care

we all know what that means
mom knows what that means

I try not to think about it
crawling under my skin
the dam keeps opening up
when I least expect it

I love my mom so much

so strong
in her mind
struggling in her body

as I get to know my way around
St. Paul's Hospital

she takes the pain

TV always on
her body shrinking
fear and courage
smiling with the sad
a wisecrack here and there

she knows

simple things taken so for granted
a bath
a visit
the family there
to help
love
and worry

bulging eyes
disbelief
at mom's bedside

one afternoon just her and I
she says she's sad today
armour down
the almost tears
I listen
hold her hand
feeling helpless

deep sorrow
deep fear
deep deep deep
spike
in my heart

I wish I could just run and keep running

my back goes out
I hobble with cane and stumble around
so trivial compared to …

then Nova Scotia
glorious distraction
I'm on the plane
glad for something
anything
to take me away

old compadres
music
memory
use the brain
these skills perfected since age fifteen
rehearse
dwell
obsess
remember
caress the songs
massage them
stretch them
plug in
go
and I'm somewhere else

it's good
very good
and my mother in the hospital is always there

exquisite distraction
thank you thank you

the road trip begins

my son is along working stage and guitars
we FaceTime my mom from the bus
and the dressing rooms

it's good to see her
she loves us
we love her

oh it's so hard to keep it together
on those calls

a message from home
no more FaceTime—why?

I don't know
but I do as I'm asked
it's eating my soul
I keep on keeping on
hoping for a miracle

then there's a break

I'm back
at the hospital
sometimes she seems to be improving
good visits

then back to the bus
after a teary goodbye
see you soon…..
the look in my mother's eyes
she knows what's happening

in her hospital bed
in palliative care

so, I focus on the music
I focus on the work….
inexorable work

two weeks pass

we're in Calgary
a day off
my family says
"don't bother coming"

but I do

from flight to mom at St. Paul's
for the final conversation

she says "good thing you came"

she knows

the last goodbye

I'm drowning in tears
as I leave the room

then like magic
back in Calgary
let's rock
because I don't want to think

the sorrow is thorough
days unrelenting

before you know it
enroute to Saskatoon

St Paul's
mom now in a coma
the hospital death lady
explaining much too pleasantly
the science and the inevitable

makes me angry
happening a lot these days

I sing to sleeping mom
hold her hand
weep

then into the car
to North Battleford
and the gig

and a darkness
settles

on
everything

finish the show

back to Saskatoon
back to the hospital

mom's soul released
at 11:11

so quiet with the machines turned off

we sit around her bed
my dad
my sister
my brother
and me
and mom

so surreal
desolate
relieved
broken

I'm all cried out

and then
I'm home

I switch on the barbed wire section of my brain
because there's one more gig
for the zombie on a mission
at the Broadway Theatre

then it's over

tour complete

I wake up Sunday morning
on another planet
cold
numb
the waves crash in

I miss my mother

I can't stop the waterfall
the slow fade
for the healing
for the strongest love
of mothers
fathers
sons
daughters
for the simple held hand
a smile
beautiful closed eyes

tenderness
bravery
courage
serenity
bond
of blood
joy
everlasting

fly free now

I love you mom

Make It Through To Sunrise

the black dog keeps on smiling
with the darkness treading water
in the lake of admonition
where all the secrets live

sleep is overrated
the night could be my friend
if I could only close my eyes
and rest

the planets hum so beautifully tonight

if I can make it through to sunrise
when the sky turns pink again
the night will disappear
broken glass will leave my eyes
if I make it through
to sunrise

memories come calling
my mind is dry
falling
I wish the heroes and the wraiths
could catch me in their arms

some things you need to figure out yourself

life and death
love and war
all the daily battles
lost and won
the closets
where they live

the stars are burning wicked blue tonight

I dream about my mother
I dream about my lover
I dream about a million lives
a million miles away

write the soul's cantata
while the angels fly in tandem
hold the light so delicate
never let it go

the universe is pouring rain tonight

if I can make it through to sunrise
when the sky spins gold again
the night will disappear
I will rest my empty eyes
if I make it through

make it through
to sunrise

The Hand from the Sky

werewolves on the highway tonight
coyotes are howling
long and wild

dreaming of aquamarine
under
a cinnamon sky

I've been here a month
I feel the weight of the world
getting lighter

small relief
from the boulders
I'm carrying on my back

the blues come and go
they're gone for a moment
the sun's coming out
the rain's crying now
the hand from the sky
is open
the hand from the sky

the phone never quits
it just keeps on ringing
like hundreds of TVs
outside in the garden
with the gnomes
and the bees

I've returned
to the place I call home
where the neighbours never notice me
and I don't notice them

a bruise never felt so good
graciously gratefully
black and blue good

the clouds wisp away
to an infinite grin

the hand from the sky
is open

the hand from the sky

Lake of Mud

I laid back
looked up at the headlights
shining on me from the ceiling

awake
with all the other worker bees
buzzing
toiling
mired
inside the hive of aural recreation

my creation

me

mountains in the sky
thickened cloudy chocolate wilderness
airwaves jammed down all the way to Mexico

I'm the one beside the pretty woman
trusting and complete
beneath the watchful eye of Mrs. Cunningham
Mrs. C

been down here before
you know now
far too often FAR TOO OFTEN
swimming in my lake of mud

slow
unhealthy

she wears a bathing cap from the fifties
black and white
sublimely moving faster than the other swimmers
in her lake of mud

anathemic rock and roll
Tiberius would have loved this place
high above the sacred city
deep inside the well
of my head

been down here before
you know now
far too often FAR TOO OFTEN
swimming in my little

lake
of
mud

Rob Roy Room

exchanging secrets in the dark
maitre'd comes to the rescue
candlelight in little boxes
all your favourite films reviewed
tolerates your drunk behaviour
loud demanding favours asked

the climax comes in one big message
SOS
I'm going crazy
all day in the Rob Roy Room
stoned familiar
shipwrecked hazy

pick those pockets one by one
don't let the inspector catch you
while you're taking out the laundry
he'll pretend he's never met you
pellet gun
looks like the real thing
never shot at any targets

have I died and gone to hell?
my memory is fading faster
praying for a miracle
that could prevent my

big disaster

wicker chairs behind the bay
there are no sharks here
so they tell me
every time I turn around
something else she's trying to sell me
funny how she hates herself
sometimes she laughs so hard she cries

plays the music in her car
with all the treble turned to zero
never wants to hear the words

who are you—where am I now?
blackout souvenir reactor
down the stairs for broken ribs
one more time

exquisite
drowning
actor

Come Across the Water

a sudden sense of urgency detected in the voice
"It's not all that important"
she says

she doesn't really mean it

she wants to run away with him
somewhere far across the ocean
wants to run away with someone
somewhere

he locks the bathroom door behind him
starts his staring competition
thin disguise of writer
over classic alcoholic

the tears roll down the beach beneath the looking glass
the sea beneath his eyes

can you come across the water?
I swear I'll never leave you
can you come across the water?

I'll wait here for a hundred years
I will not be abandoned
I refuse to be discarded
I'll always wear these medals
I never will surrender

his heart feels like an anvil
tied around his ankles
he can hear the engines of the ship above him
searching for the northwest passage
through the frozen ice

alone

now high above the earth

a moment's passion passes
in the North Atlantic sunset

he thinks he's been betrayed again
all the cards are on the table
1945 again
still fighting
knows it's over
kill the madman
KILL THE MADMAN
how could we have believed him?

damn us all to hell
I'm sorry - don't think I can keep on going
shoot me if you must
I'm lying down
upon this field of flowers
May already
smells like spring
the blood of spring already

she's on the plane
a one-way ticket

"take me to America"

come across the water
I swear I'll never leave you

come across the water
I'll wait here for a hundred years
I will not be abandoned
I refuse to be discarded

will you come across the water?

come across
for me

Junkie Pride
___

junkie pride
takes you for a pretty ride

when you die
I'll see you on the other side

junkie pride

I just want to play
my guitar
I just want to see you
as you really are

broken bones
can't leave well enough alone

the devil lied
laughing while your mother cried

junkie pride

I just want to watch my
flowers grow
instead I crawl
and scratch and scream
in here alone

saving grace
in this godforsaken place

throw it over the side

soul decider
bareback freight train rider

junkie pride

I just want to feel like
GOD again
I just NEED to be alone
with my best friend
I just want to leave
before the movie ends

I just want to feel
the way I felt before
I just want to know the truth
nothing more

I'm looking in the mirror
at a
wasted
lonely
whore

junkie pride

This Rage

this rage

why this rage inside my liquid torso?
spreads my ribs—break!! c'mon …
break already!

when it arrives it astounds

a greenish glow
the vacant committee of tentacled brainsicles
peering
iridescent

afraid
red with ire
red with salty tears

a crying little boy with clothespins on his ears
wondering where the pain came from

the neighbourhood bullies laugh
flee

however
occasionally
some years later

the cinematic scope is quite something

as the art class thug receives the unforgiving fists
from the clothespin victim

victim no more

machete in the back seat
and a memory of every wrong
rising to the surface

and
serenity prayer

in time....

this is why

I cannot drink

Send the Saints

send the saints
send the letter
let the puppies know the snow is here

some of the birds are still singing
the smart ones left

9 AM with Goat's Head Soup
this is 60

a stack of books I swear I'll read
or at least go through
or scan
or read about on the old wikaroo

and then the fear

what the hell??!!
my time is almost up - what have I done???
no one comes here and why should they?
no GREATNESS
no CITIZEN OF THE YEAR

be still
let the silence speak in raptured tongues

tinnitus in these greying elephant ears
as I turn up the volume once again
welcome to the Walk of Fame
a Christmas Carol for the new millennium—ha!

visited by at least three ghosts
while CBC News chugs away on mute

It's really all about the here and now I guess

sad diagnosis yesterday ... beautiful Lady ...
LYMPHOMA
she's hurting ... that's all I can say about that ... right now ...
so many salty tears ... come on ... STOP!

but I can't

love is precious
friends are finite
I am so sad
please
send the saints

International Superstar

he was an international superstar
standing alone at the end of the bar
he just pawned off his favourite guitar
international superstar

look at the international superstar
drunk as a skunk
trying to light a cigar
he just dumped his wife
the bank took his car
international superstar

when the ship went down
we were singing Hallelujah
when the lifeboats fell
he was drinking with the ladies

there's the international superstar
showing the waitress his surgery scar
someone call the cops
it's getting bizarre
international superstar

look at the international superstar
singing his songs in this big empty bar
no one coughed up
when they passed around the jar
international superstar

when the ship went down
we were singing Hallelujah
when the lifeboats fell
he was dancing with the ladies
when the lights went out
he was looking for the lighthouse
when the water rose
he was crying

for his mama

international superstar

Heartaches and Numbers

you roam these halls every night
the paintings all seem to be haunted

you receive what you ask for
you get all the things
you ever wanted

you're thick as a sponge full of water

making up rhymes

they all sound the same
you're just shooting pigeons

a big waste of time

rain's coming down
I'm watching it wash you

you're thick as a sponge full of water
you squeeze into jars in the kitchen
for memories as full as a camera
with pictures you never will take to the store
to develop
while you're sitting here
high
in the dark
with the world's biggest war
on your lap

dreaming of heartaches and numbers

a taste like snowflakes
on your tongue
hard rock candy
NEED TO GET SOME

remember how good
bliss can feel
tastes so good
couldn't
be
real

in a couple of days
you'll feel so much better
the shakes will wear off

now you're straighter than straight
so there are no excuses
just SIT THERE AND WAIT

you're thick as a sponge full of water

needing
begging
dreaming

of
heartaches
and
numbers

The Sadness is Strong

the sadness is strong

the waves are thick
like Alsatian syrup
when they crash

why-did-my-mom-have-to-die-why-do-I-mess-everything-up
why-am-I-such-a-pathetic-addict-why-am-I-such-a-loser???

mirror mirror on the wall

go away
crossword mellow come get me please

blue-and-pink-and-pink-and-blue
Love-the-daddy-Love-the-mother-Love-the
warm limbs of summer embrace
holding me close to the giant's enormous breast
with freshly brushed shades of wicker enamel
on the surfaces
of the atoms
in the molecules

all aboard the wave

turn on the TV
radio
computer (it's always on)
save me from my rotating grey matter

it's always on

dreaming of vodka
dreaming of cannabis
dreaming of true love

dreaming of anything
anywhere
the horse
the carriage
the honeymoon ride

in the days before credit cards
when wild beasts roamed the streets
on the AM radio band
hot
in Florida

I was the same
confused-stoned-drunken-half-measure-of-a-man
when we saw the alligator
watching the raccoons

it looked like curtains
for those screeching grifters of the everglades
in the saturated palm tree sunset

but no dinner for the reptile

now I'm back
in my room
where I write
remember
and piss away my silver years

still
the sadness is strong

Men's Wing Christmas

Saturday night
forty below
muffled voices on telephones
make those calls quick!

you know they're listening
you know who they are
is this just a bad movie??

called earlier
no go
always busy

FORBIDDEN

this is the penance
the price that must be paid
marking the days
one by one

December twenty fifth

nobody wants to see Santa Claus cry
nobody wants to see Frosty die
nobody wants to be alone tonight

but I do ...
just doing time with the fellas
in Men's Wing

merry christmas

Spaghetti Western

alarm clock ring

how you DESPISE that thing

always your enemy
infrequently your friend

this tender moment
you kiss the day hello
off to work you go
to face the wicked world

a caffeine morning
with all your FAVOURITE tunes
blasting you through the traffic
to the afternoon

spaghetti western

grain trucks go rolling by
high with the visions
of the bread they will create

hard times for lovers

better to see than do

no use in dying young
keep that gun
inside its holster

you will go riding on the range
you'll throw your troubles high into the wind

then the new day will begin

one side a garden wall
one side a waterfall
tightrope barbed wire circus
on display

just when you think
it might work out
the wind will blow
the trunk will close
both your hands
will be broken

like Don Quixote
you'll do whatever is right
you will pray tonight
under contented skies

this tender moment
you kiss the night hello
off to sleep you go
to dream of far away adventures

we will go riding on the range
we'll toss our heroes
high into the wind

then the new day will begin

The Win

hoping for that gargantuan win

then my life will be so much better
insert happy face

please and thank you
send me palm trees
send me ammunition
send me memories extracted
a stubborn tooth encumbered
by gums unyielding

automatic social weapons
aspiring to greatness

holding on by my fingernails
to
ANYTHING

GOD
thank you for great album covers
basketball shoes
and
SOBER ENERGY

I believe in
one more day
absorbing
praying
doing
the
work

for the win

Clean

kitchen table
full of old receipts and papers
a few new weeds saying hello
in my back yard
daily conversation
with my maker

it sure feels good to be clean

been a few years now
since I left the darkness
it still comes back to visit
once in a while

always about twenty minutes late
for everything I do

but it sure feels good to be clean

guitars and microphones
still fill up most of my life
words and music
still put smiles on my face
I finally figured out
how to run my own race

it sure feels good to be clean

I won't forget the past
I use it now and then
I see things different
than I ever did before
I haven't given up on love
I just know now who my real friends are

it sure feels good to be clean

all those ghosts
always scared me
now I look 'em in the eye
and say, "how ya doin' buddy?"

when the demons try to dare me
I just laugh
and say, "man you got the wrong guy"

it doesn't matter if it rains
or if it shines
because every day is a better day

when I let go
and turn my face up to the
big blue sky

it sure feels good to be clean

More Ferocious in Toronto

more ferocious in Toronto
shake the stealthy

only in dreams
never enough
of where

can't believe I'm alive tonight
"thank you—thank you very much"
with no moderation
on lubrication

slow and easy
meditation

if only it was that simple
to get some sleep

but NO
I REFUSE TO SLEEP
all of you can just
GO TO HELL

because
this is where I live now

only twenty or thirty more years left
if I'm lucky
so see you at the grocery store
I guess

maybe so

but I can still put the
PEDAL TO THE METAL
on the 401
because it's

MUCH MORE
ferocious
in Toronto

Rode In On

wake up wake up

you just won
the Stanley Cup

it was just a dream
you're still playing on the losing team

plug in plug in
turn it on
let's begin
to make this noise

send it out
to all the girls and boys

make it me make it me
be the one
who's on TV

another selfish pig

on the verge of something
really big
oh yeah

spend it all spend it all
walking over a waterfall
on a tightrope twist
whoever thought
it would come to this ...

forget you and the horse you rode in on

it's you it's you
cooking up
this toxic stew

when the ice caps melt
you'll remember how good
a cold day felt

a test a test
to see who finishes
second best

here in tiny town
they'll crush you
until
you're six feet underground

respond respond
to the scum
swimming in the pond
they're all crawling out
to see what the noise
is all about

you'll do you'll do
anything
they want you to
you smile and wave
as they drag me by the hair
into the cave

forget you and the horse you rode in on

you brute you brute
walking around
in your birthday suit
you're the patron saint
from the
Church of Zero Self Restraint

my fault my fault
I locked the money
in the vault

so safe inside
like a smile
on the lips of a wild bride

get on get on

in the morning
you'll be gone
to another place
might as well be
in outer space

another car crash
in another race

in love in love
it's the thing
you've been dreaming of

the war's been won
it's time to load up
another big old gun

so...
forget you and the horse you rode in on

Unsuccessful Son

where is the farm I left?
where are the songs I learned?
did I smoke them all away
in wisps of white roller skates
and plastic doll hair?

great big EMPTY
with a scone blue tint
easter egg blue
robin egg blue
Miles blue
free range teeth chattering mind numbing
blue

there you have it

depression and the thing we shall not speak of
on a stick

this is the pandemonium and sad explanation
of the
unsuccessful son

a bobsled track inside my head
with those sneaky Soviet bobsledders
from when I was a kid
milling about
weighing the odds
of defecting successfully

define defection—I dare you

a natural human condition
deflect
then defect
there must be a word for this in Latin

is the romance of this age a victim
of stunted teenage velocity?
you bet baby

no questions asked
in a smoky May alley
where the rough folks ride their own bobsled tracks
every
single
day

like the sad sixties Soviets

the unsuccessful son

Lifetime Plan

a lottery ticket
25 bucks
this is my LIFETIME PLAN

fasten the seatbelt
or don't
you could be THROWN CLEAR
saving your life
yep

money enter stage right
exit stage left
head hung down
financial riptides
complete with jellyfish who sting
sharks who leave you maimed and bleeding
out on the edge of some tranquil beach that really looks great
on TV

so I'm barricading
prevaricating
looking at a
GIANT NUMBER SIXTY

trés chic
so ... long ... ago
and of course
60 is the new 40

tell that to my little black bag lungs
or my pre-medieval knees
all part of the plan

Who Cares (Unemployed)

it was a history of the movies
a sermon on the science
of making people laugh and cry
and sing
out
loud

the sad parts brought the tears on
the bad parts made me wince
until indifference hit me so hard
that I have not returned since

who cares

it was the best damn book I ever read
it really got inside my head
I could not think of anything else
for quite
a long
time

it had to be a true story
no one could make up that stuff

I'd lived it
I felt it
I could not get enough

but you can't believe everything you read
you can't believe everything you see
I can't believe this has happened to me

who cares
it doesn't really matter
who cares
if you get what you're after
who cares

I never thought I ever really cared

he said
"you'll never work in this town again
there's no place here among these men

for people who won't listen to
every word I say"

I replied, "WHO DIED AND MADE YOU KING??"
at least that's what I meant
but I realized at the final second
I had not paid the rent ...

so I bit my tongue
laughed it off
like I so often do
I've been through all this before
and so have all of you

all of us

who cares
if I go to work on Monday
who cares
if I get to sleep in Sunday
who cares

it doesn't really matter anyway

who cares

Too Long

demon in my skeleton
electrified again
black clouds rolling in bigtime

cue the thunder
save the whale
cut the balloon string on the helium sunrise
for the all night fight is about to begin

when the waves lap up
tongues consuming
flickers
failures

here we are
frowning upon the gnashing teeth
of the muscled beast inside

the power of pleasure

a painfully
long
slow
death
of
syllables
and
interminable
pauses

too long

Sagging Sunday

my cynicism
replaced by the wheels of industry
pounding the plains
like a drunken sailor on shore leave

now we MUST BE HAPPY
because
just because

this empty house
furnace off (new filter needed)

sagging
Sunday
afternoon

"I'm so sick of everything"
I say
with zero conviction

much too antiquated
to muster even melancholy

listening to the click click of the clock
at the stillness
of my grandfather's desk

is this IT?

no TV
answers ahoy

I'm a big blank stare
at an empty wall
on a sinking
sagging
Sunday

Mouse in a Hole

there's a mouse
in a hole
digging
his own grave

there's a child
with her mother
teaching her
how to behave

there's her brother
in the classroom
he really
doesn't give a damn

there's his buddy
his name is Alphonse
he's been worshipping
the son of sam

there's the teacher
with a ruler
bored
with all the people in his life

there's the principal
in a daydream
in love
with his best friend's wife

there's the best friend
on a bender
with his business
going downhill

there's the waitress
who thinks he's wealthy
she's moving in
for the kill

a policeman
looks in the window
he's jealous
becoming quite upset

there's the radio
in the police car
predicting crimes
that haven't happened yet

there's his partner
who's looking forward
to the rock
he's gonna smoke tonight

there's his girlfriend
who he lives with
she knows
that something ain't right

something
ain't
right

there's a tourist
with a camera
eating french fries
and a big shake

there's the mother
with her children
teaching them
their newest mistake

then there's Alphonse
working at the counter
of this leading
hamburger chain

there's the teacher
with the principal
and his best friend
running in out of the rain

in comes the waitress
with the policeman
he's off duty
feeling pretty good

there's his partner
who tried to get straight
with his girlfriend
who did all that she could

then there's this other guy
with a shotgun
in the parking lot
dreaming about hell
because
he knows
he's going to go there
when he uses
his last shell

he slams the car door

he walks up

to the front door
of the restaurant
with a smile

then he drops dead
on the pavement

never dreaming
all the while

that there's a mouse
in a hole

digging
his own
grave

there's a father
with his son
teaching him
how to
behave

something
ain't
right

there's a mouse
in a hole

digging
his
own
grave

New Day

stand like a statue
with the world balanced on the back
of the new day

pick the piece of the pie you want
slice it up for the thick and thin
on the new day

give the man the weak ones
he will make them strong
on the new day

South Carolina
on the beach with a tidal wave
on the new day

selling South America
big money and the ozone gone
on the new day

make the list
make it fit
do the heist
fifty-fifty split
on the new day

a simply stunning

same old

new day

Surrounded By Love

left on the doorstep
baby in blue
crying and wiggling
ready to live

took in by the nuns
raised as a holy man
grew to be tall
filled with
vast
love

he turned eighteen
went out on the ocean
hauling up ropes
climbing the crow's nest
one of the crew
on a ship with no name
privateers plundering
the Spanish Main

conscience conflicted
he was a good boy
life brings changes

VIOLENT
SWIFT

he jumped ship
in the north land
made for the mountains
with small provisions

needful of warmth
red beard
muscles

heart
on the hillside

he came to a cave
where he met a woman
living wild
on the edge of the timber

her hair was dark
as the sky
in a summer storm
her eyes were blue
as the sea
in the harbour

they shared a fire

the fire
stayed
burning

babies were born
one after another
two girls and boys
they lived on the mountain
hunting the deer
eating the greens
like the people
who had lived there
before them
for a thousand years

then came the soldiers
with weapons of silver
started out friendly
but they
wanted more

greed led to blood

blood led over the mountain
to the valley
where no one
had ever been before

into the wilderness they fled
hungry and broken

they came to a spring
full with bubbles
swirling churning

and a small shining man
on a branch
on a tree
smiling down
he said
"here lies love—the water is warm"

the man and the woman
gazed at each other

inhaled the stillness

caressed the silence

entered the water
children in arms
faith in their hearts
hope in the cradle
of gentle Mother Earth

when they awoke
the peace was upon them

the world anew
in the fountain of youth

forever

surrounded by love

Sending Love

a lighthouse in a tempest
will not be denied
a candle in a window
a beacon in the night

in the hour of tribulation
in my time of need
I give myself to you completely
I give you all of me

I'm sending love

an ocean will not separate
my soul from your soul
time and space will not detain me
from the heart I hold

there's a strength inside of us
for the message to be sent

from me to you
from you to me
from two to one
across the sea
above the clouds
beyond the stars
into the sun
eternal and complete

I give it all to God

I give it all to you

I'm sending love

Redberry (love song to a lake)

flipping through the pages
acting half your ages
making crazy promises you'll keep

seems you've seen this all before
all you need—nothing more
never good to look before you leap

sing until the sun comes up
filling up your coffee cup
half awake and smiling at the sky

pelicans
hummingbirds
all the best songs have no words
all the finest singers need to fly

she's a redberry
the kind you'd like to marry
redberry

I'm in love

anarchists
dadaists
scientists
biologists
won't know what it means to wear a frown

when they walk these woods
on summer days
learn about the ancients' ways
it feels like they're in heaven looking down

safe inside the conscious mind
tired of working overtime
search the sky for any kind of sign

try your best to let it go
forgetting everything you know
wake up in the morning feeling fine

she's a redberry
a princess on the prairie
redberry

I'm in love

Macramé
___

What-they-say-what-they-say??
two hundred miles an hour
every single day

I'm up
OK
I'm down
OK
I'm evolving

really?

when the lock is locked
bolt is bolted
walls caving in
lungs are

s-q-u-e-e-z-i-n-g from the TENSION

just sit
breathe
sit
breathe

macramé

Sizzle Magoo

a friend to all
with blurry vision

not Jim Nabors

it's
that guy

father of James in
RWAC

him

the name currently escapes me
so
I guess he wasn't all that FAMOUS

LA is kinda nice
it's summer here all year long

is it Jim?

yes I know I could look it up on my phone
but

testing my memory

need more ginkgo

hmmm

sizzle magoo

Let the Love In

it's pineapple season down here on the farm
one hundred degrees—it's getting quite warm
we're happy and healthy
ready to pop
so open the doors of the chopper
let's do the drop

the ghost in the house is quite active tonight
she tries not to frighten but still causes fright
when the chandelier sways
the earth starts to shake
it's time for the show to begin
let the moon in

"you're welcome" she said
but I hadn't said "thank you"
you better be good
or the lady might spank you
we talk about lawyers
we talk about treatment
we talk about coffee
and chocolate
and eating
and drinking

yes
drinking

let the truth in

casino with all the big money and bright lights
cigarettes glowing
all smoky tonight
she never played slots
so I threw in a quarter
she was good luck
'cause I came out ahead
on the border

I wanted a drink but I couldn't stop playing
it feels good to win every once in a while
we got in the car
drove into the desert
LA down the road
the Grand Canyon
way too far

we rolled down the windows

looked out at the stars

we let the love in

Flora Vista

just look at you
covered in sun
I'm counting freckles on your cheek

warm desert wind
blows your hair across your eyes
I swear you get more beautiful each day

it sure feels good to be alive

California sure looks good on you

I picked an orange right off a tree
it tasted
just like heaven

you caught me laughing
you're laughing too
I want to laugh with you forever

are you an angel?

sometimes I swear
I'll see you sprout wings
take to the air

am I just dreaming?
is this for real?

when you say
"I know exactly how you feel"

out here it looks like we're on the moon
except for a cactus
or two

in our lawn chairs
Mojave sun
let go the old
bring in the new

it sure feels good to be alive

California sure looks good on you

climb on
we'll go for a ride
anywhere you want
I'll go with you

anywhere you want

Diving In So Deep

breathe
breathing you in
scent of your skin
I'm swimming in you

steam
soaking you through
beautiful you
I'm confessing

it always opens with a look
holding me hostage
with your eyes
then the touch
then the kiss
then we're

diving in so deep

smooth green lush
velvet to touch
in a garden of you

soul touching a soul
sacred to hold
your heart in my hands

scarlet anticipation now
I'm in a universe
of absolute perfection
in your eyes

diving in so deep

giving you everything I am
giving you everything I have
the sun the moon the ocean
deep

a wild Arabian stallion
charging through the surf
towards you

the waves come crashing now
our lungs
kissing each other
while we dream

diving in so deep

For Certain

blue eyes
pink lips
sitting across from me
tonight

indigo heaven
lavender light

space walk
slow talk

rippling milky way
in sight

stars in the window
paint you
just right

the last day of august
feels like the first
I only need you
in the peach of the dawn
this is for certain

you're happy
you're smiling

light as a bee buzzing home
to hive

heavenly
golden
serenely alive

I only need you
holding my soul

this is for certain

Sweet Sweet Love

whisper whisper
take me to Spain

kiss me
kiss me
kiss me
again

I will

whisper
your name

September
October
November
December

you're here
I love you
now and forever
sweet sweet love

you are all
you are everything
the universe
the birds that sing

the planets smiling
welcoming
golden hymns
you bring

I open my arms
I open my heart
I open my soul
to you

I drink from the well
of your
sweet sweet love

skin on skin
lips on lips
sugar at the touch
of your fingertips
sweet vibration
sweet sweet love

whisper whisper
take me to Spain
Las Vegas Nevada
back home again
come inside my soul
come on in

I'm shaking

from the
sweet sweet love

quivering
soaking
steaming

in the
sweet
sweet
love

Before You Leave Canada

before you leave Canada
I have something to say
I'd like you to listen
then you can go on your way

you never liked hockey
you never liked bacon
you always said it was way too cold
I agreed
but you still kept complaining

you can have palm trees
I'll keep my pines
you can have money
that all looks the same
I kinda like the queen's face
on mine

before you leave Canada
for the red white and blue
remember
somebody's waiting
back home in the snow
for you

I love America
like I love my sister
we don't hang out that much anymore
sometimes I miss her
but if I was in trouble
she'd be there in a flash
if I needed a shoulder to lean on
a ride somewhere
or even some cold, hard cash

oh Canada …

you put on your makeup
you're wearing new clothes
the taxi is waiting
you're ready to go
I gave you maple leaf kisses
I kept your toes warm
I plugged in your car every night
so you wouldn't have to go out
in a freezing snow storm

before you leave Canada
just kiss me goodbye

I swear it's the last time
you'll ever see
a Canadian cry

The Moon The Stars and You

wind on the water
songs of the waves
a beautiful ending
to a beautiful day

you're snuggled beside me
the world is just right
feels like we're waltzing
in heaven tonight

the moon the stars and you
the sky so big
your eyes so blue
the moon the stars and you

lights in the distance
ships on the bay
whispering to us
asking to stay
sand on our toes
salt in our hair
you kiss me and smile

heaven's right there

with the moon the stars and you

Drop You in the Water

old John the Baptist
standing out in the wild
saw Jesus coming
he took His hand and smiled

"I'm gonna drop you in the water
gonna make you swim
gonna drop you in the water
I believe that you are Him"

when you're dragging that dead weight
down a gravel road
gonna need someone to help you
with your heavy load
it'll hit you like a freight train
rolling down the track
when the Lord puts the hammer down
you won't look back

gonna drop you in the water
gonna make you swim
gonna drop you in the water
you will follow Him

a hundred miles an hour
down the interstate
you might as well just be
standing still
you won't be late ...

the river is deep
the river is wide
you can see the Lord waiting
on the other side

you jump right in
your bones get cold

keep your eyes focused
save your soul

you cannot feel the bottom
your legs go free
the current starts to take you
you just want to scream

your arms start moving
you're kicking your feet
arms start moving ...

gonna drop you in the water
gonna make you swim
gonna drop you in the water
you will follow Him

Jesus is Gonna Help Me

I'm digging deeper
I'm trying harder
than I've ever tried before
I'm calling out for someone to help me
no one's listening except my Lord

I'm not alone now in this big world
I will find redemption here
I know
Jesus is gonna help me
make the shadows disappear

I've been in trouble
so many times now
with all my earthly wants and needs
I have been travelling down this highway
paved with sorrow—lined with greed

when temptation starts to follow
and the devil says "come on over here!"
I know
Jesus is gonna help me
make the shadows disappear

a thousand angels on my shoulder
will carry me back home
when the night is dark and cold
I'll never be alone

there may be good times
there may be hard times
skies may be cloudy—may be blue

I have my saviour here beside me
His love will see me through

we'll walk in sunshine
we'll stride through rainbows
see the horizon pure and clear
I know
Jesus is gonna help me
make the shadows disappear

Gospel

boy on a Greyhound looking for truth
staring out the window with nothing to lose
tracks on his arms
gin on his breath
he just needs a place to rest
gospel

woman in the garbage looking for food
man walks by says something rude
she just smiles
keeps on digging
voices in her head keep on singing
gospel

it is what it is—ain't no more
Jesus hung out with the lepers and the whores
good things come to those who wait
say hello to love
goodbye hate
gospel

put on your hard hat—time to go to work
down in the deep where the demons lurk
trying to stay on the straight and narrow
feel it in your bones
feel it in your marrow
gospel

I could load a lorry—I could load a gun
I could run away or I could just run
up to the top of the highest hill
to talk to God
I'd be talking there still
gospel

Sunday morning—bells so loud
walking outside on the edge of the crowd

doors are open
there's a place for me
sitting right next to the Christmas tree
gospel

thank you Lord for another fine day
clouds disappeared—went on their way
I'm still here
you are too
thanks for everything you do
gospel

thanks for the sun

thanks for the moon

it is what it is—ain't no more
keep on knocking
He'll open up the door
good things come to those who wait
say hello to love
goodbye hate
gospel

Asleep in the Loving Arms of God

sun comes up
sun goes down
valley throws its
weight around
every morning

tide comes in
tide goes out
stars wake up
go about
their business

the beds are made
we're all awake

safe in the hills
safe in the mountains
safe at home

breathe in the air
swim in the moonlight
fall asleep in the loving arms
loving arms of God

river runs
down to the ocean
trading the fresh
for the salt
in slow motion

resting our heads
on the shoulder
time doesn't matter
no need for younger
or for older

the birds are singing
they're all awake

safe on the plains
safe in the desert
safe at home

whisper your secrets
soak in the sunshine
fall asleep in the loving arms
loving arms of God

I have a dream
every night
I'm in a pool
full of love
and light

hold up the palms of your hands
to the sky

safe on the shore
safe on the ocean
safe at home

breathe in the love
close your eyes now
fall asleep in the loving arms
loving arms of God

For The Love Of A Word

for the love of a word
a sail to be set
a song to be sung
an EPIC to be told
a place at the table
set to be sold
to the highest bidder

bleak stare across the vast lunch counter savannah
"menu unknown"

a joke
then perhaps a clue
in one more mystery
for the diner sleuth

however

truth be told
honest as the day is long
word is kept

patience letters symbols
taken for granted
mysteries
should be mysteries

knife through butter
profound resolve
straining compassion …

key in lock
turn of switch
world awaiting
smile luminescent

through tears I witnessed
wonderful greenest of green
in the spaces close
and in between

magic words nestling

holding fast

for the love of a word

God's Daughter

girl with the moon in her hair
birds
butterflies
buzzing
halo invisible
I know it's there

pink
transcendent
green
ripening
twirling

purple umbrella in the rain
singing at the fountain
beaming through the window

stick out your tongue
drink up the drops

some run for shelter
others dance

sprite
eyes closed
twilight sun
fluorescent water
intensely in love
with
life

God's daughter

Oh, to be madly, intensely in love with life …

Jay Semko

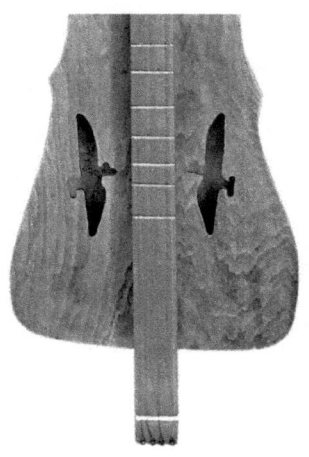

Albums

MOUSE (1995)

"Mouse" was my first solo album after the extended hiatus of The Northern Pikes in 1993. The Pikes regrouped in 1999 for a Canadian tour to promote "Hits & Assorted Secrets", the first of three "Best of Pikes" albums to be released.

This album was recorded with my pal, the late Les Cantin, as engineer and co-producer. I really enjoyed the freedom of being able to utilize pedal steel guitar on many of the tracks. Les did a fantastic job of capturing where I was at artistically at the time and I was accompanied by some great musicians from Saskatoon on this record.

The lyrics from the album "Mouse" appearing in this book are:

Adventure on My Breath - a defiant ode to independence and the road after suffering the loss, at the time, of The Northern Pikes

Mouse in a Hole - a stream-of-consciousness story of interconnection, coincidence and the potential for tragedy

Lake of Mud - slogging through depression on a seemingly endless trip

Who Cares (Unemployed) - getting fired by a film industry bully after an "artistic disagreement"

REDBERRY (2006)

After "Mouse", I concentrated on music for film and TV. The series "Due South" changed my life and I began a whole new career. Although the Pikes recorded two albums of new material in 2000 (Truest Inspiration) and 2003 (It's a Good Life), Redberry was a return to recording my solo material after a long hiatus from that world. The album was recorded mainly in Saskatoon with Ross Nykiforuk, who toured and recorded with the Pikes from 1991-93. We billed our production team as The Cosmic Twins. Redberry features guest vocalists Serena Ryder, Theresa Sokyrka, Andrea Menard, and Brianna George (now Brianna Burtt). I love the fretless bass played by Skip Kutz on this album. As with all my solo albums, I had great musicians on this album, who were fun to work with, and these extremely talented female vocalists were a nice counterpoint to my lower vocal range.

The lyrics from the Redberry album appearing in this book are:

Rode In On - a socio/political stab at myself and my world at the time

New Day - another socio/political stab inspired by news of a tsunami

Spaghetti Western (originally titled *Another Day* on the album) - trying to do the right things to get through the day while fighting adversity and depression

Come Across the Water - doomed love and desperation - inspired by a book I read about the confusion and sadness in Europe following the end of World War II

Rob Roy Room - addicted to alcohol and spending days in a hazy bar

Redberry (A Love Song to a Lake) - I had a cabin at Redberry Lake in Saskatchewan—home of the Redberry Lake Migratory Bird Sanctuary and a place of fond memories with my family during an otherwise challenging period of my life.

INTERNATIONAL SUPERSTAR (2008)

This was my first "fully sober" solo album. I was seeing the world through new eyes when I did this album. I went to a treatment centre in Quebec in late 2006, relapsed shortly after, then sobered up in March 2007. There were many co-writes on this album with some great songwriters in Nashville and Canada. The album was recorded and mixed quickly in Saskatoon with Ross Nykiforuk, and features some nice guitar work from Jay Buettner and some fine pedal steel from Warren Rutherford.

The two songs from this album appearing in this book are:

International Superstar - a semi-autobiographical drunkalogue…..yep that was me

Jesus Is Gonna Help Me - the first gospel song I wrote. I entered it in the 2008 John Lennon Songwriting Contest and it was the runner up in the Gospel category. It was written in a time of desperation—I asked for, and received, much needed help from my higher power and subsequently created this song.

JAY SEMKO (2010)

Produced by Jay Buettner and recorded mainly in Abbotsford and Vancouver, BC, this album was recorded "Nashville-style"—live off the floor with fantastic studio musicians. This was a new and interesting recording experience for me at the time. The songs were mainly co-writes with songwriters in Nashville and Canada creating a fine sounding record. The two songs from this album appearing in the book are:

Before You Leave Canada - international heartbreak inspired by other's misfortunes—but I got a cool song from it. Tongue-in-cheek but still gets me misty eyed when I sing it in concert. I was nominated for Songwriter of the Year in the 2011 Western Canadian Music Awards for writing this song.

Drop You in the Water - the second gospel song I wrote was a smoking bluesy music track recorded live off the floor. I entered it in the international Independent Songwriting Competition and it was a finalist. I guess I have a bit of a knack for spiritual songs that are straight ahead biblical.

FORCE OF HORSES (2011)

This album was mainly comprised of co-writes and songs originally recorded for the "Jay Semko" album sessions. Although no songs from this album appear in this book, the album won the 2012 SCMA (Saskatchewan Country Music Association) Award for Roots Album of the Year.

SENDING LOVE (2012)

Recorded at MCC Recording Studio in Calgary, Alberta and co-produced with Johnny Gasparic, this album triggers fond memories. I played all the keyboards on the record—a first for me—and there is beautiful guitar work throughout the album from Russell Broom. The album was nominated in the 2012 Western Canadian Music Awards for Roots Solo Recording of the Year, the same year The Northern Pikes were inducted into the Western Canadian Music Hall of Fame.

I guess this album is pretty much all about love. The songs from this album appearing in the book are:

Sending Love – love ... spiritual and timeless

For Certain - the mystery and certainty of true love on a summer night

Sweet Sweet Love - sensual spiritual physical

The Moon The Stars and You - a lullaby for a starry night

FLORA VISTA (2014)

This album was mainly written in California when I had an unexpected extended stay there ... the songs just started happening. This album won the 2015 SCMA Award for Roots Album of the Year. It was engineered and co-produced by Randy Woods in Saskatoon. For me, this album is California. The songs from this album appearing in the book are:

Clean - a sense of serenity after weathering the storm of addiction

Flora Vista - a desert love song inspired by the street of the same name in Palm Springs, California

Let the Love In - inspired by an earthquake and a road trip through Nevada and California while trying to stay clean and keep it all together

Junkie Pride - a song written while I was in a treatment centre in Quebec in 2006 and finally released on this album in 2014.

Asleep in the Loving Arms of God - intended to be a song of serenity and comfort. I believe God can be found anywhere, but especially in nature. I sang this song to my mom when she was in a coma at St. Paul's Hospital in Saskatoon before her passing. I will always remember singing it to her softly in the quiet room.

Surrounded By Love - an epic tale of history repeated ... love will survive.

NEVER SENT (2018)

Recorded with Randy Woods in Saskatoon, this album garnered me a nomination as Spiritual Artist of the Year in 2020 in the Western Canadian Music Awards. Definitely a spiritual slant to this record, the songs from this album appearing in the book are:

Gospel - say hello to love - goodbye hate

Make It Through To Sunrise - addicted, depressed and trying to hang on … with a spooky bluesy thing happening

The Hand From the Sky - originally written for the "Blues From the Herts" compilation album to support the SANE Mental Health Charity in the UK in 2015. I updated the recording for the "Never Sent" album, attempting to keep faith while I was in the depths of depression.

Diving In So Deep - love can conquer all … so dive on in.

HEARTACHES AND NUMBERS (2010) BY SEMKO FONTAINE TAYLOR

This album was recorded and released by the trio Semko Fontaine Taylor, comprised of myself, Kim Fontaine and David J. Taylor

Heartaches and Numbers was the title track - waiting, jonesing, trying to stay cool when inside you're freaking out - addiction personified in this song

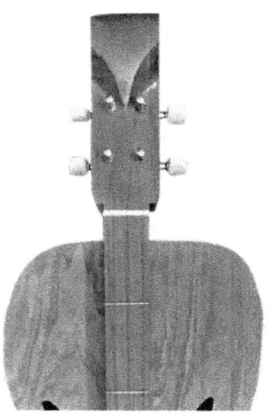

*If you are in distress and feel like you may harm yourself or others ...
call someone.
The relief and cathartic nature of sharing our feelings cannot be underestimated.
You are not alone.*

CALL SOMEONE
ANYONE
YOU ARE LOVED

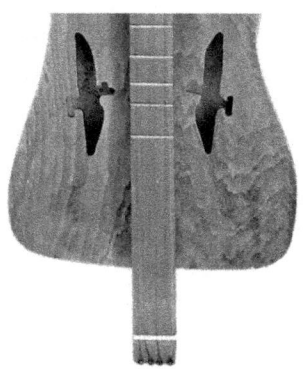

www.ingramcontent.com/pod-product-compliance
Lightning Source LLC
Chambersburg PA
CBHW070509100426
42743CB00010B/1794